ABRAHAM, MOSES, JESUS, and MARY

ABRAHAM, MOSES, JESUS, and MARY

Divine Revelations from the Quran

Thasneem Ahmed

Paper & Quill Press
Cypress, CA

PAPER & QUILL
PRESS

Paper & Quill Press,
Cypress, CA

To the children of Abraham:
May there be love, happiness, and
blessed friendships between us.

CONTENTS

PREFACE

The Quran is full of stories detailing the lives of Abraham, Moses, Jesus, and Mary. Many of the significant events that took place during their lifetimes are shared so that we may be inspired, guided, and comforted by their faith, courage, and perseverance. In the Holy Quran, there are hundreds of verses about these blessed individuals, and their stories are arranged in a manner that mostly emphasizes different life lessons. As such, the stories of Abraham, Moses, Jesus, and Mary are not presented in the Quran in chronological order but are rather woven throughout the entire text like a beautiful tapestry. Some of the verses are similar to those found in the Torah or in the Bible. And some verses are new revelations, never revealed before in any of the previous holy scriptures.

My hope with this simple compilation is to give readers a glimpse of the profound love and honor bestowed by God upon these four noble human beings, and to inspire them to live life with the courage, faith, and dignity with which these individuals lived their lives.

There are two ways this book can be approached. The first is to read it from beginning to end for an overview of how the Quran speaks of

Abraham, Moses, Jesus, and Mary. The second approach is to read the chapters that feel more significant to you and perhaps to your own faith (i.e. Moses, Jesus, etc.). Whichever approach you choose, may this book bring you inspiration, peace, and blessings.

In the following pages, short prefaces are included before each translation to help the reader understand the general context of the verses. These are given in a slightly more bolded font as is shown here.

The Quranic verses are formatted in a stylized font as shown here, and are listed with their corresponding surah (chapter) number followed by the verse number(s). For further reference or to understand a particular verse better, you can easily look up any Quranic translation in print or online.

May God's blessings be upon Abraham, Moses, Jesus, and Mary, and may our shared love and reverence for each of them bring us together as the family of Abraham.

And We bestowed upon him [Abraham], Isaac and Jacob, and ordained among his offspring Prophethood and the Scriptures [the Torah to Moses, the Gospel to Jesus, and the Quran to Muhammad], all from the descendants of Abraham, and We granted him his reward in this world, and verily, in the Hereafter he is indeed among the righteous. 29:27

◆ ◆ ◆ ❖ ◆ ◆ ◆

ABRAHAM
The Friend of God

The story of Abraham is one of unwavering faith and complete devotion to God. The Quran shares Abraham's tests and trials, and his story is divinely instructed to be told to future generations.

And convey unto them [the people] the story of Abraham. 26:69

In the sixth surah (chapter) of the Quran, we are told of a youthful Abraham and the interactions he had with his father, Azar, one of the high priests of the time. Not only were Azar and the people idol worshippers, but they also worshipped celestial beings. Abraham deeply longed to know God, and God graciously turned toward him and showed him the mysteries of the universe. After Abraham had seen the truth, he tried to show his father and the people the error of their ways through reason and the demonstration of logic.

Remember when Abraham said to his father,

Azar, "Do you take idols as gods? For surely I feel that you and your people are in manifest error and have gone astray." And thus, in this way, did We then show Abraham the kingdom, the power, and the laws of the heavens and the earth, so that he might have knowledge and be of those who are certain in faith.

And when the night came with her covering of darkness, he [Abraham] saw a star, and he said, "This is my Lord." But when the star faded away in the morning light, [Abraham] said, "I love not that which fades away." And when he saw the moon rising in its entire splendor, he said, "This is my Lord!" But when it set, Abraham said, "Unless my Lord grants me guidance, I shall surely be among those who go astray." Then when he saw the sun rising in all its resplendent and majestic glory, he said, "This is my Lord! This is the greatest of all!"

But when it too set, [Abraham] said, "O my people! I disown all that you worship beside God and I am free from your guilt of giving partners to God. For me, I have turned my face firmly and truly as a true believer towards Him, who created the heavens and the earth, and never shall I give partners to

God!" 6:74-79

With gentleness and humility, Abraham tried to convince his father of the error of idol worship, but his father's reaction was harsh and severe. Despite this response, Abraham continued to pray for forgiveness for his father.

And remember when [Abraham] said to his father "O my father! Why worship that which cannot hear, nor see, and cannot profit thee anything? O my father! Behold, there has indeed come to me a ray of knowledge such has never yet come unto thee. Follow me, and I will guide you to a path that is even and straight. O father, why do you worship Satan? Do not worship Satan, for he was disobedient to God, the Most Gracious. My dear father, I fear that a punishment from God, the Most Beneficent, may befall you and make you a companion of the devil."

He answered, "Do you reject my gods, O Abraham? If you do not stop this folly, I will indeed stone you to death. So go away from me and be gone for a long time!" And Abraham said, "Peace be upon you. I will ask for forgiveness for you from my Lord. Verily, my Lord is the Most Gracious." 19:42-47

Abraham also tried to convince his towns-people of the follies of idol worship.

Remember when Abraham said to his father and to his people, "What are these idols to which you cling to with so much devotion?" And they answered, "We found our forefathers worshipping them." He said, "You and your forefathers were in clear and manifest error and have gone astray." They asked, "Is this the truth that you are bringing to us? Or are you one of those who jest?" And Abraham replied, "It was in fact your Lord, the Lord of the Heavens and the Earth, who created all that is in existence, and brought everything into being.

And I am one of those who bears witness to this truth." 21:52-56

Despite the difficulties that Abraham faced due to his father and his people, he held fast to his faith and was determined to keep working in God's path. Abraham came up with a plan to try to show the people the futility of their idol worship.

And he thought to himself, "By God, I shall most certainly bring about the downfall of your idols as soon as you have turned your backs and gone away!" And then he broke them all to pieces, all save the biggest of them, so that they might turn to it when they return. [And when the people saw what had happened] they cried out, "Who has done this to our gods! Surely he must be a wicked one and one of the evil doers." And some of them said, "We heard a youth speaking of our gods with scorn. His name is Abraham."

They said, "Bring him here before the people, so that they may bear witness against him!" [And when he came] they demanded to know, "Was it you who did this to our gods, O Abraham?" And he said, "Obviously, someone has done it. Why don't you ask the one that is left, the biggest one of them all, to tell you who did this?" Then they [those who were not as keen on idolatry] turned towards them and said, "Surely, you are the one doing wrong." And then they, crestfallen and confounded with shame, said, "You know full well that these idols do not speak."

Abraham said, "So then why do you worship something besides God, something which can neither help you, nor can do you any harm? Fie upon you and fie upon all those that you worship instead of God. Will you not understand and use your own sense *of reasoning?"* 21:57-67

Some of the townspeople realized their error. However, most of them became even more enraged. The people, including members of Abraham's own family, turned against him and tried to kill him by throwing him into a fire. But God rescued Abraham and delivered him to a blessed land.

But the people cried out in anger, "Burn him alive and avenge your gods if you are a people of action!" But We commanded, "O Fire! Be you cool and comfortable, and a source of peace for Abraham." And then they desired to harm him and declared war upon him, but We caused them to suffer the greatest loss and made them the losers. And We rescued him and delivered him and [his brother's son] Lot, to the land, which We have blessed for all nations and times to come. 21:68-71

The king, Nimrod, was an arrogant tyrant in the land and the Quran mentions the confrontation Abraham had with him.

Art thou not aware of the king [Nimrod], who argued with Abraham concerning God, simply because God had granted him kingship? Lo! Abraham said, "My Lord is He who grants life and deals death." The king replied, "I too grant life and deal death!" And Abraham said, "Verily, God causes the sun to rise in the East, so then you cause it to rise in the West." Thereupon, he who was bent on denying the truth was dumbfounded. And God does not guide people who deliberately do wrong and who are unjust. 2:258

Abraham was devoted to God and to worshipping only Him. The close relationship they had was demonstrated when Abraham asked God to show him how He brought things to life.

And behold! Abraham said unto his Lord, "My Lord, show me how You give life to the dead?" And God asked, "Do you not have faith?" And Abraham said, "Yes, I believe, but I ask to see in order to reassure and ease my heart and to be stronger in faith." And his Lord said, "Take then four birds, and teach them to be obedient to you. Then slaughter them and then cut their bodies into pieces, mix them and place a portion of them separately on every hill surrounding you. Then summon them to you. And [God will bring them back to life and] they will come flying back to you swiftly. And know that your Lord is Mighty and Wise." 2:260

Abraham prayed to God for a child, and God heard his prayer and granted him a son through Hagar (also known as Hajirah in Islam). Hagar had become Abraham's second wife, and when their son was born, he was named Ishmael, meaning "And God hears and answers" as Ishmael was the answer to Abraham's prayer. The Quran tells us of Abraham's prayer as well as of the test of obedience that was given to both Abraham and his son.

And Abraham prayed, "O My Lord, bestow upon me the gift of a son, one who shall be of the righteous." So We gave him the glad tidings of [Ishmael] his first-born, a gentle son. And when his son was old enough to share in his father's endeavors, Abraham said, "O my dear son, I have seen in a dream that I must sacrifice you. Tell me, what do you think and what is thy view?" And he replied, "O my Father, do that which you have been commanded. By the will of God, you will find me patient and steadfast." Then, when they had both surrendered themselves to God, and he [Abraham] had laid his son down on his forehead [for the sacrifice]. We called out to him, "O Abraham! You have already fulfilled the purpose of that dream!"

Thus indeed, do We reward the righteous. For Behold! Truly, this was indeed a tremendous trial. And We gave him in exchange a great and noble sacrifice. And left for him to be remembered by generations to come in later times. Peace be upon Abraham! Thus do We reward the righteous and the doers of good. For verily, he was truly one of Our believing slaves. 37:100-111

And make mention in the Scripture of Ishmael. Lo! He was always truthful in his promise, and he was a messenger of God, a prophet. And he enjoined on his family prayer and almsgiving, and was one in whom his Lord was well pleased. 19:54-55

Later, Sarah was also blessed with a child and Abraham was given the gift of a second noble son, Isaac. The conversation that took place amongst the angels, Abraham, and Sarah is depicted in Surah Al-Dhariyat (surah fifty-one titled "The Winds that Scatter") of the Quran as well as in several other surahs.

Has the story reached you, of the honored guests of Abraham? Behold! When those [heavenly messengers] entered his presence and said, "Peace." He [Abraham] replied, "Peace." And thought, "These are a people unknown to me and seem unusual, and are strangers in this land."

Then he turned quietly to his family and household, and brought forth a fattened and roasted calf. And then, placing it before them, he [waited, and then] said, "Will you not eat?" And when he saw that his guests would not eat, he became apprehensive of them, (but) they said, "Fear not." And they gave him the glad tiding of the birth of a son who would be endowed with deep knowledge.

Thereupon his wife, waiting nearby, came forward with a loud cry and striking her forehead, said in astonishment, "A son to a barren old woman like me?" And they said, "Your Lord has spoken. And He is the Most Wise, the All-Knowing." 51:24-30

And his wife stood laughing with wonder and happiness whereupon We gave her the glad tidings of the birth of Isaac and after Isaac, of a blessed grandson Jacob. 11:71

And We gave [Abraham] Isaac and Jacob, and ordained among his progeny Prophethood and Revelation, and We granted him his reward in this life; and verily, in the Hereafter, he is indeed [in the company] of the Righteous. 29:27

God's blessings upon Abraham and Abraham's praise of God:

"All praise is due to God, who has bestowed upon me, in my old age, Ishmael and Isaac! Behold, My Lord indeed hears all prayers." 14:39

God's commandments to the descendants of Abraham:

Say, "We believe in God, and in what has been revealed to us and what was revealed to Abraham, Ishmael, Isaac, Jacob, and the Tribes, and in the Books given to Moses, Jesus, and to all the prophets, from their Lord. We make no distinction between one and another among them, and to God do we submit." 3:84

And remember in the divine scripture, Abraham. Behold! He was a man of truth, a Prophet. 19:41

And God was so pleased with Abraham that

He took Abraham unto himself as His friend and gave him the noble and honored title "Khalil" meaning the friend of God.

And who is there, that has a better religion than one who submits his will to God, who does good, and who follows the creed of Abraham, a man of pure faith? And God took Abraham for a friend. 4:125

Abraham in Islam

The Prophet Muhammad looked to the great patriarch Abraham not only as a messenger of God but also as his forefather, as Muhammad's lineage is traced back to Ishmael. The difficulties Muhammad had with the pagan Arabs were in many ways similar to the ones that Abraham underwent with his people, as both communities were devoted to their idols. The early Arabs worshipped nearly 360 idols, many of which were made of clay, wood, or stone. These statues were housed in the Kabah in Mecca, and when the religion of Islam was established, they were brought out of the Kabah and formally destroyed.

From 1,400 years ago to present times, many

of Abraham's and his family's actions are symbolically reenacted as part of the annual Islamic ceremonial rituals during the (once-in-a-lifetime) pilgrimage called Hajj. These rituals include the circumambulation around the Kabah, the sacrifice of the lamb, Hagar's quest for water, and the stoning of the devil. In this manner, the pilgrims (called Hajjis) performing their Hajj in Mecca are not only being reminded of Abraham, but are extolled to follow his example. This yearly recommitment to faith and reenactment of Abraham's actions by millions of Muslim pilgrims reinforces the high stature of Abraham in the Islamic faith. At the same time, it also reinforces the family-like closeness the Muslim people share with their Jewish and Christian brethren.

Abraham's Mosque
(Masjid Al-Khalil)

The Mosque of Abraham (also known as Masjid Al-Khalil) is considered the fourth holiest mosque in the world and is located in the city of Hebron, Palestine. It is believed that Abraham, Isaac, Jacob, and his son, Joseph, as well as their wives, are buried in the caves underneath the mosque.

The entranceway to Abraham's Mosque.

Source: www.travelpalestine.ps

The interior prayer hall in Masjid Al-Khalil.

Source: www.travelpalestine.ps

MOSES
From a Slave to a Prince

Of all the prophets, the one mentioned most frequently in the Quran is Moses. The life of Moses is presented in exquisite detail, with honor and reverence, and is introduced with a simple question to the reader.

Has the story of Moses reached thee? 79:15

The Quran begins by telling us the great evil that was taking place in the land during the time when the children of Israel were in bondage and their sons were being slaughtered. Moses's mother was one of the believing women, and God granted her divine inspiration to save her son.

We now share with you some of the story of Moses and Pharaoh, setting forward the truth for the people who believe. Behold! Pharaoh had elevated himself and had become high and mighty in the land,

and had divided its people into castes. One group [the children of Israel] he persecuted; he slaughtered their sons and spared their daughters, for he [Pharaoh] was indeed an evil-doer. But it was Our will to bestow Our favor upon those who were being oppressed in the land, and to make them leaders in faith and to bestow upon them a noble inheritance.

And so We revealed to the mother of Moses, "Nurse thy child, but when you fear for him, cast him into the river, but fear not nor grieve, for We shall restore him to you, and We shall make him one of our message-bearers." 28:3-5, 7

God tells us of the distress and anguish of the mother of Moses during that time, and how He strengthened her and guided her so that she might be reunited with her child.

But on the morning of that day, the mother of Moses became troubled with an aching void, and she would have indeed disclosed all about him had We not endowed her heart with enough strength to keep alive her faith [in Our promise]. And so she had said to his sister, "Follow him," and the girl watched him from afar, while they who had taken him in were not aware of it. And We ordained that he refused to nurse at first, until [his sister came up and] said, "Shall I show you the people of a house that will nourish him and bring him up for you and be sincerely attached to him?" And thus did We restore him to his mother, so that her eye might be gladdened, and that she might grieve no longer, and that she might know that God's promise always comes true—even though most of them know it not. 28:10-13

The surah continues on to the story of Moses as a young adult. A turning point is described when Moses confronts one of Pharaoh's people to save a Hebrew slave. While defending the slave, Moses accidently kills Pharaoh's man and becomes a wanted fugitive in the kingdom.

Now when Moses had reached the age of maturity, and was firmly established in life, We bestowed upon him wisdom and knowledge, and the ability to judge [between right and wrong]. Thus do We reward those who do good.

And one day he entered the city at a time when most of its people were resting unaware of what was going on in the streets, and there he encountered two men fighting with one another— one of his own people [a Hebrew slave], and the other being one of their oppressors and enemies. And the one who belonged to his own people cried out to him for help against him who was one of his enemies—whereupon Moses struck him down with his fist, and [thus] brought about his end.

But then he said to himself, "This is Satan's doing. Verily, he is an open foe leading man astray." And Moses cried, "Forgive me, My Lord! For I have sinned against my own soul." And God forgave him, for He is the Most Forgiving, Most Merciful.

Moses said, "O My Lord! I (vow) by all the blessings which Thou has bestowed upon me, never again shall I help those who are lost in sin." The next morning, he [Moses] came into the city fearful, cautious, and hesitant. When Lo! The one who had cried for his help the day before, called aloud for his help again. Moses said to him, "Truly, you are indeed a quarrelsome fellow in plain error!" Then, when he decided to seize their common enemy and was about to lay his hands on him, their enemy said, "O Moses! Is it your intention to kill me as you killed a man yesterday? You only wish to become a violent tyrant in this land and not be one of those who set things right!"

And then a man came running from the farthermost end of the city, and said, "O Moses! The chiefs are deliberating upon thy case with a view to killing thee! Be gone and flee for your life, for verily, I am one of those who wish you well and give you sincere advice!" Upon hearing this, he [Moses] fled from the city, full of fear. And he prayed "My Lord, save me from a people who are unjust and wicked." 28:14-21

God granted Moses direction as he desperately prayed for help. By steering Moses toward the far away land of Midian, God guided Moses to a place where he would be secure and protected. And it was there that he would receive training for the next stage of his life.

Then, as he turned facing the land of Midian, he said, "It may well be that my Lord is guiding me to the right path."

And when he arrived at the waters of Midian, he found there a whole tribe of men watering [their flocks]. And at some distance he came upon two women who were keeping back their flock. He [Moses] asked them, "What is it that troubles you?" They answered, "We cannot water our animals until the shepherds take back their flocks, and our father is an elderly man." So he watered their flocks for them, then he withdrew into the shade and prayed, "O My Lord, truly I am in desperate need of whatever good that You may bestow upon me."

Some time afterwards, one of the damsels came back to him, walking bashfully. She said, "My father invites you so that he may reward you for having watered [our flocks] for us." So, when he [Moses] came to him and narrated the story of his life to them, [their father] said, "Do not fear. You have escaped from an evil people, and you are now safe from the wrong-doers."

And said one of his two daughters, "O my Father, hire him, for surely he is the best of men that you can employ—strong and worthy of trust." And [after some thought] the father said, "I intend to wed one of my two daughters to you on the condition that you serve me for eight years, but if you stay and complete the service for ten years, it will be as a kindness from you. For I do not want to impose any hardship on you, (indeed) you will find me, God-willing, righteous in all my dealings." And Moses replied, "Thus shall this agreement, between me and you, whichever of the two terms I fulfill, let there be no compulsion upon me. And let God be a witness over what we say." 28:22-28

Moses helped care for the flocks of sheep. After his time of service had been completed, he left with his family to settle in a new place. It was during this time that God called Moses to Mount Sinai. This event was one of the most miraculous moments in the history of mankind, and Moses was given the honor of speaking directly with God.

And when Moses had fulfilled his term and was traveling with his family in the desert, he perceived a fire in the distance, on the slope of Mount Sinai. He said to his family, "Wait here. Behold, I perceive a fire far away, perhaps I may bring you from there some tiding, or [at least] a burning brand from there so that ye may warm yourselves." But when he came to the (fire), a voice was heard from the right bank of the valley, from a tree in hallowed ground, "O Moses! Behold! I am God, the Lord of all the Worlds." 28:29-30

The Quran explains in detail the majestic conversation that then took place and how God elevated Moses to prophethood by virtue of the signs he was being given. With these miraculous signs, he was then given the task of returning to Egypt to confront Pharaoh.

"Verily, I am Your Lord! Take off your shoes, for you are in the sacred valley of Tuwa. I have chosen thee (to be my Apostle), so listen to what is being revealed. Verily, I am God, there is no God but I, therefore serve Me and perform the prayers of My remembrance. The Hour is coming, though I choose to keep it hidden, so that each soul may receive its reward, by the measure of its endeavors. Therefore, do not let anyone who does not believe in it and follows his own desires, distract you from it, and so bring you to ruin and let you perish."

"And what is that you have in your right hand, O Moses?" He [Moses] said, "It is my staff, whereupon I lean on it, beat down the leaves to feed my sheep with it, and I have other uses for it too." 20:12-18

And then God commanded, "Throw down your staff." But when he [Moses] saw it moving, writhing like a snake, he withdrew back in terror and did not dare to return again. And it was said unto him, "O Moses. Come near and fear not. For Verily, you are of those who are secure [in this world and in the next]. Now, place your hand inside of your shirt upon your bosom, and it will come forth shining white [without any harm to you], and draw your hand close to you and do not be afraid. These shall be two signs from Thy Lord to Pharaoh and to his chiefs. For truly they are a people rebellious, defiant and depraved.

Go now unto Pharaoh, for he has indeed transgressed all bounds." 28:31-32, 20:24

Moses accepted God's command immediately, and also asked God to aid him with his brother Aaron.

And Moses said, "O My Lord, I have killed a man of theirs and I fear that they may put me to death. And my brother Aaron is more eloquent in speech than I. So I ask that he be sent with me to support me, as a helper. For I fear that they may accuse me of falsehood, and reject me." 28:33-34

And God said, "Granted is thy request, O Moses. We shall strengthen you with your brother to help you and will bestow upon the both of you such power, that no one will be able to harm you. By virtue of these and Our Signs, you two shall triumph as well as those who follow you." 20:36, 28:35

God then reassured Moses, informed him of the favors that had been bestowed upon him since childhood, and confirmed his ordainment.

"And indeed, We had already conferred a favor upon you another time [before]. Behold! We sent to thy mother by inspiration, this message, 'Place him (the child) in a chest and throw it into the river, and there upon the river will cast him upon the shore. And one who is an enemy unto Me and an enemy unto him will adopt him.' And thus did I spread My own love over you Moses in order that you may be raised under My eye, raised by My will."

"And [We favored you] when your sister went and said, 'Shall I direct you to someone who will be responsible for him?' So We restored you to your mother that she might be content and not grieve. And when you did kill a man, We delivered you from great distress and tried you with a heavy trial. Then you stayed a number of years with the people of Midian.

Then you came here according to the fixed time, which I ordained, (for you) O Moses. And I have chosen you for Myself." 20:37-41

God commands Moses and Aaron to go to Pharaoh and prepares them for their task.

"Go, thou and thy brother, with My Signs and slacken not, either of you, in keeping Me in remembrance. Go, both of you, to Pharaoh, for he has indeed transgressed all bounds. And speak to him with a gentle word, that perhaps he may accept admonition or [at least] be filled with apprehension." They said, "Our Lord, indeed we are afraid that he may hasten to do evil to us, or that he may transgress all bounds (against us)." He said, "Fear not. For verily, I am with you both, hearing and seeing (everything)." 20:42-46

In the Quran, God reaffirms several times the special status given to Moses as a prophet and a messenger of God.

And We inspired other messengers whom We have mentioned to thee, as well as messengers whom

We have not mentioned to thee, and God spoke His Word unto Moses directly. 4:164

Thus Indeed! Did We send Moses with Our messages, signs and a manifest authority from Us. 40:23

Verily, We have sent unto you (O mankind) a messenger to bear witness over you, just as We had sent a messenger (Moses) to Pharaoh. 73:15

MOSES
From a Prince to a Prophet

The Quran tells us of Moses' elevated status from a prince of Egypt to a prophet of God, and of the difficult work that he and his brother Aaron were asked to do with Pharaoh.

And mention in the Scripture the story of Moses. Indeed, he was purified and specially chosen, and he was a messenger (of God), a Prophet. 19:51

And We sent forth Moses and his brother Aaron with Our Miracles and clear proofs and a manifest authority (from Us) unto Pharaoh and his chiefs, but they behaved with contempt and insolence, for they were an arrogant group, who wanted to (only) glorify themselves. 23:45-46

The Quran shares the conversation that Moses had with Pharaoh, and the tests and trials he endured in the royal court, in powerful detail.

And Moses said, "O Pharaoh, Verily I am a Messenger from the Lord of all the Worlds. I come under the condition that I speak of God only that which is the truth. I have come unto you indeed with a clear sign from your Lord. So let then the Children of Israel depart with me." Said Pharaoh, "If you have brought us a sign, then produce it and bring it forth if what you say is true."

And at this, Moses threw down his staff and behold, it became a live serpent for all to see. And he drew forth his hand and behold, it was shining white for all to witness. The chiefs among them said to Pharaoh, "This is indeed a sorcerer of great skill and one who is well-versed in magic!" They said, "His plan is to drive you out of your kingdom." So Pharaoh asked them, "So what then is your counsel?" They answered, "Let him and his brother wait for a while, and send into the cities heralds with summons for every skillful sorcerer to come to you."

And so the magicians came unto Pharaoh and asked, "Shall there will be a reward for us if we win?" And he [Pharaoh] responded, "Yes, not only reward, but more. You shall be among those who are near to me." So they asked, "Moses! Will you cast your spell first, or shall we cast ours first?" And Moses answered, "You cast first." And when they cast down their spells, they mesmerized the people and showed great sorcery and struck them with awe and terror. And they produced a mighty enchantment. 7:104-116

And in his heart, Moses became apprehensive. 20:67

And then We inspired Moses, "Throw down thy staff!" And Behold! It (became a serpent and) swallowed up the creations of their sorcery and deceptions. And thus the Truth was established, and all that they had done collapsed in defeat. And Pharaoh and his people were vanquished and were utterly humiliated. 7:117-119

Pharaoh was furious that Moses had defeated his sorcerers and even more enraged that the sorcerers were now submitting themselves to the God of Moses. He and his chiefs planned their revenge on Moses and his people.

And the sorcerers fell down to the ground in prostration, saying, "We believe in the Lord of the Worlds! The Lord of Moses and Aaron!" And Pharaoh said, "How dare you believe in Him without my permission! This is surely a plot you have all planned to drive the people out of the city! But soon you shall face severe consequences and my revenge! Know that I will cut off your hands and feet on opposite sides, and I will then crucify you all!" And the sorcerers replied, "We will then be returning to Our Lord. And you take your vengeance on us only because we have come to believe in the signs of Our Lord when they came before us. Our Lord, pour upon us patience in this adversity and cause us to die as believers who have surrendered to You."

And the royal chiefs asked Pharaoh, "Will you allow Moses and his people free to commit mischief in the land? And to abandon you and our gods?" And he [Pharaoh] replied, "We shall slay their sons in great numbers and shall spare only their women, for verily we hold tremendous power over them." 7:120-127

The Israelites became fearful of Pharaoh's rage and looked to Moses for guidance and support. Moses turned to God and inspired his people to stand firm in faith.

Said Moses to his people, "Turn to your Lord

for patience and constancy in adversity. For the earth belongs to God, and He gives it as a heritage to those of His servants as He wills, and the future belongs to the righteous." And they responded [in grief], "We were persecuted and suffered before you came to us and now we are made to suffer hurt after you have come to us." And he responded, "It may well be that your Lord may soon destroy your enemy and make you the inheritors of the land, and then see how you conduct yourselves." 7:128-129

But none, save a few believed in Moses [and they held back] for fear of Pharaoh and his chiefs, lest they should be persecuted. And verily, Pharaoh was an arrogant tyrant on the earth. And was indeed one of the evil-doers who transgressed all bounds. And Moses said, "O my people! If you believe in God, then in Him alone, place your trust and submit your will to Him." And they said, "We put our trust in God. Our Lord, do not let us suffer at the hands of these wicked tyrannical people. And deliver us, by Thy Mercy, from those who reject the truth." 10:83-86

Moses instructed his people to build houses for worship and prayer, to help strengthen their faith.

And (thus) did We inspire Moses and his brother, "Build some houses in Egypt for your people, and make those and your homes places of worship. And establish regular prayers. And give glad tidings to those who believe!" 10:87

Pharaoh persisted in his scathing haughtiness and deceptions.

And Pharaoh proclaimed among his people, saying, "O my people! Is not the kingdom of Egypt mine? And [witness] these rivers flowing underneath [my palace], do you not then see? Am I not better than this [Moses], who is insignificant and contemptible, and can hardly speak clearly? Why are there not golden bracelets upon him, nor angels sent with him as companions?" Thus he [Pharaoh] persuaded his people to make light [of Moses], and they obeyed him; for truly they were a rebellious people. 43:51-54

God sent punishments and plagues upon Pharaoh's people as a warning for their arrogance and as a means for them to receive admonition. But they did not take heed of these lessons.

And Indeed! We punished Pharaoh's people with years of draught and scarcity of fruits and crops, so that they might take it to heart and receive admonition. And they said [to Moses], "Whatever of the signs you bring forth to deceive us with, we shall never believe you!" Thereupon, We let loose upon them floods, [plagues of] locusts and lice, and frogs, and of water turning into blood. Distinct signs (all), but they gloried in their own arrogance, for they were people lost in sin. 7:130, 132-133

God gave the Egyptian people some respite when they relented and promised to free the Israelites. But they repeatedly broke their promises. And after a set period of time, God commanded Moses to take his people and leave Egypt.

They would say, whenever the punishment struck them, "Moses, pray to your Lord for us by virtue of the promise He has made to you. If you relieve us of this plague, we will believe you and let the Children of Israel go with you." But, when We relieved them of the chastisement and gave them a fixed period [for them to fulfill their promise], lo and behold! They broke it. 7:134-135

And there came a time when We inspired Moses, "Go forth with my servants and travel by night, for surely you will be pursued." 26:52

When Pharaoh realized that the Israelites had escaped, he commanded his troops to pursue and destroy them. The Egyptian army chased the Israelites and caught up with them at the edge of the Red Sea (or what may also be known as the "Sea of Reeds"). Moses and his people were trapped between the army and the sea and panic rose within the people as they realized the dire situation.

And then Pharaoh sent heralds unto all the cities [bidding them to summon his troops and proclaim], "These slaves are indeed a small contempt-ible band of fugitives. And Verily! What they have done has enraged us! And we are a people united with a large army and well-prepared!" 26:53-56

And so they [Pharaoh and his soldiers] pursued them at sunrise and caught up with them. And as soon as the two multitudes of forces came within view of each other, the followers of Moses cried out, "Lo! We are certainly sure to be overtaken and defeated!" 26:60-61

Moses held strong to his faith and prayed. And God, in all His majesty and glory, opened the sea for the Israelites and delivered them to safety, while causing Pharaoh and his companions to drown.

And Moses said, "Nay Indeed! My Lord is with me, and He will soon guide me." Then We revealed to Moses, "Smite the sea with thy staff!" Whereupon it parted, and each side became as a huge towering mountain, vast and firm. And We caused the pursuers to draw near to the place and to follow them. And We delivered Moses and saved all those who were with him. 26:62-65

And We inflicted Our retribution upon them [on Pharaoh and his companions], and We caused them to drown in the sea because they denied and rejected Our Revelations and had been heedless of them. 7:136

Behold! In this there is indeed a sign! And yet most of men will not believe. 26:67

The Quran tells us of the interaction Moses had with God on Mount Sinai and of the gift of the stone tablets containing God's laws. With this gift came also the responsibility of adhering to God's laws, and God showed Moses and his people the consequences that had befallen those who disobeyed.

And then We appointed for Moses thirty nights on Mount Sinai. And We added to them ten, whereby the term of forty nights set by His Lord was fulfilled. And Moses said unto his brother Aaron, "Take thou my place among my people, and act righteously, and follow not the path of the spreaders of corruption and wrong-doing." And when Moses came to the appointed place, his Lord addressed him. And [Moses] said, "My Lord, show me Thyself, that I may gaze upon Thee." And God said, "By no means can thou see Me directly, but gaze upon the mountain! If it abides firm in its place, then shall thou see Me." And when His Lord revealed (His Majesty) to the mountain, it came crashing down. And Moses fell down in a swoon. And when he woke, (Moses said) "Glory unto God! I turn unto Thee repentant, and I am the first of true believers!"

Said God, "O Moses! Behold, I have raised thee above all people by virtue of the Messages, which I have entrusted to thee, and by virtue of My Speaking unto thee. Hold fast, therefore, unto what I have given thee, and be among the grateful." And We ordained for him in the tablets (of Law) all manner of admonition and instruction, everything all clearly illuminated. And (We said), "Hold fast unto them with all thy strength, and enjoin thy people to hold fast to the most goodly rules therein. Soon I shall show you the homes of those who were immoral and wicked [and how they now lie desolate]." 7:142-145

And unto Moses, We gave the Scriptures, complete for those who would do good, an explanation of all things, a guidance and a mercy, that they might believe in the meeting with their Lord. 6:154

God honored Moses and his followers, and they were given special status as being among those who have received divine guidance. And among the people of Moses are those who are commended for guiding with the truth and for being just.

Indeed, unto Moses and Aaron, We granted Our Criterion as a standard by which to discern the true from the false, and as a guiding light and a reminder for those who are God-conscious. 21:48

And among the people of Moses, there is a community who guide with the truth, and who establish justice. 7:159

Moses in Islam

The name of Moses is mentioned in the Quran more than 130 times, more than any of the other prophets' names. It is through this emphasis and these revelations of Moses and of the Children of Israel that the Quran gives Muhammad and the Muslim community spiritual lessons.

Shortly after the Prophet Muhammad migrated to Medina, he learned that the local Jewish tribes were celebrating their escape from Egypt with fasting and prayers, and that Moses himself had done the same. The Prophet Muhammad, in solidarity with the practice of Moses, then chose to also fast on that day and commanded his followers to do so as well. And, by doing so, to commemorate the day that God had saved the believers from tyranny. From that year onward, Muslims (primarily the Sunni Muslims) have celebrated this day, called Ashura, with fasting, remembrance, and gratefulness for God's mercy toward the believers. Ashura falls on the tenth day of Muharram (the first month in the Islamic calendar), and many Muslims fast for one to three days in observance of this special holiday.

In the Holy Land, between the cities of Jerusalem and Jericho, is the Mosque and Tomb of Moses. The exact site of Moses's burial place is unknown, but it is believed that he is buried near this location in the surrounding desert.

The Mosque of Musa (Moses). The complex consists of
the mosque and prayer hall, the maqam (tomb), and a
large inner courtyard surrounded by over 120 rooms.
To the side of the complex lies a cemetery for the
local Palestinian Muslim community.

© 2014 Mahmoud Illean

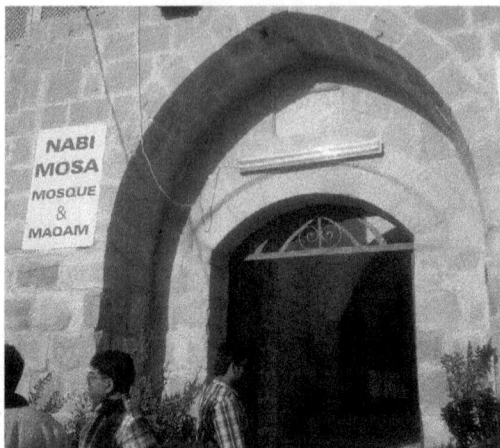

The entrance to the Mosque and tomb (Maqam) of Moses.
© 2014 Thasneem Ahmed

The Tomb of Moses.
© 2014 Thasneem Ahmed

The interior courtyard with dome-capped rooms.

© 2014 Habeeb Hasseem

JESUS
Christ the Messiah

The Quran tells us of Jesus in relation to the Virgin Mary, a young woman who obeyed God and was blessed with piety. It was through her that God gave us Christ the Messiah.

And remember her who guarded her chastity. We breathed into her new life through Our Spirit (Angel Gabriel), and We made her and her son a sign (of grace) for all of mankind. 21:91

And remember when the angels said, "O Mary! The Lord giveth thee glad tidings through a Word (Be!) from Him, of a son who shall be known as Christ the Messiah, son of Mary, held in great honor in this world and in the world to come, and he shall be one of those brought near unto God. He shall speak unto the men from the cradle, and as a grown man he shall be [of the company] of the righteous." 3:45-46

Jesus, the son of Mary, was sent as a mercy to mankind and was blessed with many miracles never before given to any of the other prophets.

And We sent forth Jesus, son of Mary, to follow in the footsteps of those earlier prophets confirming the truth that remained in the Torah, and We bestowed upon him the Gospel, wherein there is guidance and light and an admonition unto those who are God-conscious. 5:46

"Lo!" God (shall) say, "O Jesus, Son of Mary! Remember the blessings which I bestowed upon thee and thy mother, how I strengthened thee with holy inspiration [the Holy Spirit] so that thou may speak unto men from infancy and as a grown man in maturity. And how I taught thee the Scripture and Wisdom, the Torah and the Gospel. And Behold! How thou did make out of clay the figure of a bird, by My Consent, and then how did thou blow into it and it became a living bird, by My Consent. And how thou did heal him who had been born blind, and the leper, by My Consent. And how thou did raise the dead, by My Consent and how I did protect you from those among the Children of Israel from harming thee when thou came unto them with all evidence of the truth. And when those of them were persistent in denying the truth and were saying, 'This is clearly nothing but deception, and mere sorcery!' " 5:110

Jesus was sent with clear signs and wisdom to clarify matters that the people were arguing over.

When Jesus came with clear proofs and signs [of God's Sovereignty], he said, "I have come unto you with wisdom and to make plain some of that on which ye dispute. So keep your duty to God and fear Him, and obey me. For God is my Lord and your Lord. So worship Him, this is the Straight Way." 43:63-64

The message that Jesus brought was to confirm the truth that was within the Torah, to ease some of the restrictions that had been placed upon the Israelites, and to remind the people to follow the ways set down by God.

"And I [Jesus] have come confirming that truth which is within the Torah and to make lawful unto you some of that which had been previously forbidden to you. I have come unto you with a sign from your Lord, so fear God, and obey me. Verily, God is my Lord and your Lord, therefore worship Him (alone), for that is the Way that is Straight." 3:50-51.

God tells of some of the gifts given to His messengers, and of Jesus who was strengthened with the Holy Spirit. Additionally, the Quran tells us how the people, despite seeing clear evidence of the truth, still disbelieved.

And some of these messengers, We have endowed more highly than others, among them were some as were spoken to directly by God [Himself]. And some He has raised yet higher. And We gave unto Jesus, son of Mary, all evidence of the truth, and strengthened him with the Holy Spirit. And if God had so willed, succeeding generations who had followed those apostles would not have opposed one another after all evidence of truth had come to them, but as it was, they did take divergent views, and some of them attained faith, while some of them came to deny the truth. Yet, if God had so willed, they would not have contended with one another, and God does what He wills. 2:253

Many of the miracles that Jesus performed are told to us in the Quran. One such beloved miracle

occurred when the disciples asked Jesus for a table spread with food from God.

Behold! Remember when I inspired the disciples to believe in Me and in My Messenger. They had answered, "We submit and we bear witness that we have surrendered ourselves to God as believers." And Lo! The disciples said, "O Jesus, son of Mary! Could thy Lord send down unto us a table from heaven spread with food?" Jesus answered, "Be conscious of God, if you have faith." And they said, "We only wish to eat thereof and satisfy our hearts, and to know that thou has indeed told us the truth, and that we ourselves may be witness to a miracle."

And Jesus, son of Mary, said, "O Lord, Our Sustainer, send down for us a table spread with food from Heaven, so that it may be a feast for us, for the first of us and for the last of us, and a sign from Thee. Give us sustenance, for Thou art the Best of Sustainers." 5:111-114

Jesus was loved by the people, yet some of the Israelites rejected him and were harsh in their mistreatment of him. The plotted to kill him, but God was aware of all their schemes.

And when Jesus became aware of their refusal to acknowledge the truth, he asked, "Who shall be my helpers in God's cause?" And the white-garbed ones replied, "We shall be thy helpers in the cause of God! We believe in God, and bear thou witness that we have surrendered ourselves unto Him." And they said, "Our Lord! We believe in what Thou has revealed, and we follow this messenger. And make us one with all those who bear witness to the truth."

But they (the disbelievers) contrived and schemed (against Jesus), but God brought their scheming to an end, for God too planned. And God is the best of planners.

Behold! God said, "O Jesus! Verily, I shall take thee and raise thee to Myself, and clear you [of the falsehoods] of those who disbelieve, and I shall place those who follow thee far above those who are bent on denying the truth unto the Day of Resurrection. In the end, unto Me you all must return, and I shall judge between you with regard to all those matters upon which you were in dispute." 3:52-55

Jesus will return once more to this world, and his arrival will be a sign of the end of times.

And indeed (Jesus) shall be a Sign for the coming of the Hour of Judgment, therefore have no doubt (about the Hour), but follow ye Me [Your Lord], this is the Straight Way. And let not Satan turn you aside. Lo! He is an open enemy for you. 43:61-62

Jesus's lineage is through Isaac, and all of the prophets through Ishmael and Isaac were virtuous, blessed, and held in high regard.

And say, "We believe in God, and in that which has been bestowed from high upon us, and that which has been bestowed upon Abraham and Ishmael, and Isaac and Jacob and their descendants, and that which has been bestowed upon Moses and Jesus, and that which has been bestowed upon all the other prophets by their Lord. We make no distinction between any of them. And it is unto Him that we surrender ourselves." 2:136

Jesus in Islam

Jesus is deeply loved in the Muslim world and his high status as being among the chosen ones of mankind is confirmed in the Quran. Although Muslims and Christians differ in some viewpoints (for instance, the worship of Jesus as a deity), both share many similar religious beliefs, including:

- Jesus was born to Mary who was a virgin when she conceived him.
- Jesus was aided by the Archangel Gabriel.
- Jesus was given the gift of the Gospel.
- Jesus performed many miracles with God's permission.
- Jesus ascended to heaven.
- Jesus is known as the Messiah.
- Jesus will return to this world near the end of times in what is commonly known as the Second Coming of Jesus Christ.

The Prophet Muhammad himself has said, "Both in this world and in the Hereafter, I am the nearest of all the people to Jesus, the son of Mary."

It may come as a surprise to some to know that from the very beginning of the Islamic faith in the Arabian Peninsula, there has been a deep friendship and an abiding love between the people of

Jesus and the followers of Muhammad. When the Muslims were tortured and persecuted in Arabia, a small group of them escaped into Abyssinia (Ethiopia) to seek shelter. The noble king was a Christian and was known for his fairness and justice. The pagan Arabs sent a convoy to convince the king to return the Muslims to Arabia, claiming that they were runaway slaves and rebels. But the wise king gave a hearing to both sides and, after doing so, gave the persecuted Muslim refugees sanctuary and protection in his kingdom.

There is a wonderful, Academy Award-nominated movie called The Message in which this historical event (as well as the story of Islam) is beautifully captured. This 1977 movie stars two-time Academy Award-winner Anthony Quinn. In the film, after hearing the arguments, the king steps toward the Muslims and, in a moving demonstration of regal authority, draws a line in the sand with his staff and says, "The difference between us and you is no bigger than this line." And then turning to the Arab convoy, he says, "Not for a mountain of gold will I give them up to you!"

It is one of the most powerful and inspiring moments not only in the movie, but also in Islamic history.

On the other side of this friendship is the trust that the Christian community has placed in the Muslims in Jerusalem. Muslim custodians are entrusted with the keys to one of the most sacred sites in all of Christianity: The Church of the Holy Sepulchre. This is the site where many Christians believe Jesus was crucified, buried, and then rose again. Inside this hallowed church, several denominations (Catholic, Armenian, Greek, Ethiopian Orthodox, Coptic, and Syriac) occupy space, each with their own specific prayers and rituals. With a spirit of shared brotherhood, the responsibility for opening the church and maintaining the keys lie with two Muslims families. And these two families have guarded and protected the keys and the church for centuries.

The Church of the Holy Sepulchre.

© 2014 Habeeb Hasseem

Inside the main hall of the Church of the Holy Sepulchre.

© 2014 Thasneem Ahmed

The stairway leading to the hill upon which Jesus
is believed to have been crucified.

© 2014 Thasneem Ahmed

MARY

The Honored Mother of Jesus

God establishes the noble lineage of Mary and tells us of the prayer made by her mother.

Behold! God raised Adam and Noah, and the family of Abraham and the family of Imran above all of mankind, all descendants and offspring of one another. And God hears and knows all things. Behold! Remember when the wife of Imran said, "My Lord, behold unto Thee, I have dedicated that which is in my womb, to be devoted to Thy service. Please accept this from me. Lo! Thou and only Thou are the All-Hearing and the All-Knowing." But when she had given birth to the child, she said, "My Lord! Lo! I have given birth to a female child." And God had been fully aware of what she would give birth to, and fully aware that no male child could ever be like the female. "And I have named her Mary. Verily, I seek Thy protection for her and for her offspring against Satan, the outcast, the evil one." 3:33-36

Mary was raised under the protection of God. And the Quran tells us of the things unseen and of the priests who cast lots to see who would become the guardian of Mary.

And thereupon graciously did her Lord accept her. He made her grow in purity and beauty. To the care of Zachariah she was assigned. And whenever Zachariah visited her in her sanctuary, he found her provided with food and sustenance. He would ask, "O Mary, whence came this unto thee?" She would answer, "It is from God. Lo! God provides sustenance unto whom He pleases without measure." 3:37

And the angels said, "O Mary! Behold! God has chosen you and made you pure, and has raised you above all of the women of the nations of mankind. O Mary, be devoutly obedient to Thy Lord, submit yourself in prostration and bow down with those who bow down in worship." And this is part of the tidings of the hidden events of the things unseen. We now reveal unto you by inspiration for you were not with them when they cast lots with quills [to determine] which one of them should be the guardian of Mary, and charged with her care. Nor were you there when they disputed and argued about her. 3:42-44

God sent His decree and blessed the Virgin Mary with an honored son.

And remember when the angels said, "O Mary! The Lord giveth thee glad tidings through a Word (Be!) from Him, of a son who shall be known as Christ the Messiah, son of Mary, held in great honor in this world and in the world to come, and he shall be one of those brought near unto God. He shall speak unto the men from the cradle, and as a grown man he shall be [of the company] of the righteous." And she asked, "O Lord, how shall I have a son when no man has ever touched me?" The angel answered, "Thus it is, such is the will of your Lord. God creates what He wills, when He hath decreed a matter, He but only says 'Be!' and it is. And God will teach him the Book and the Wisdom, the Torah and the Gospel." 3:45-48

The Quran tells us in more detail of the miraculous moment when the Angel Gabriel appeared in front of Mary and breathed into her something of God's inspiration.

And remember through this divine scripture, Mary, when she withdrew from her family and sought seclusion [for prayer and solitude] to an eastern place. She had placed a screen to screen herself from them. And then We sent her our angel, and he appeared before her as a grown man in all respects. And she said, "I seek refuge from thee with God, the Most Gracious, come not near me if you fear your Lord!" And the angel said, "I am but only a messenger from your Lord, to announce to you the gift of a holy son, endowed with purity."

And she said, "How can I have a son when no man has touched me and I have not been unchaste?" And he replied, "So it shall be. This is what Your Lord has said, 'It is easy for Me. And it may be that we may make him a revelation for mankind and a blessing and a mercy from Us.' It is a matter ordained." 19:16-21

And Mary, the daughter of Imran, who had guarded her chastity, We breathed into (her) of Our Spirit, and she testified to the truth of the words her Lord and of His Revelations, and she was among the devoted ones. 66:12

The Quranic revelations share the events leading to the birth of Jesus Christ, the esteemed son of Mary.

And in time she did conceive him, and then she withdrew with him to a remote distant place [to Bethlehem valley]. And the pains of childbirth drove her to the trunk of a palm tree. And she cried out in anguish, "Oh, would that I had died before this and been forgotten, long and utterly forgotten and out of sight!" Thereupon a voice called out to her from beneath the palm tree, "Grieve not. Thy Lord has provided a rivulet running beneath thee, which runs at your feet. And if you shake the trunk of the palm tree towards you, it will deliver fresh ripe dates for you. So eat, drink, and cool thy eyes and be gladdened and at peace. And if you do see any human being, say, 'I have vowed a fast to God, the Most Gracious, and this day I will not enter into any conversation with any man.'" 19:22-26

When Mary returned to the people with her baby, they were astonished and reprimanded her. But baby Jesus spoke to the people from the cradle so that they might hear the truth.

And in time, she brought the baby to her people, carrying him in her arms. They said, "O Mary! You have brought something truly strange and unheard of and hard to believe!" But she [Mary] made a sign to them and pointed to her child. They said, "How can we speak to one who is a babe in the cradle?" Whereupon, the child spoke and said, "Behold! I am indeed a servant of God. He has given me revelation and has ordained me a prophet. And His blessings are upon me wheresoever I may be. And He has enjoined upon me to establish prayer and to give alms to the poor for as long as I live. And He hath made me to be (with kindness and piety) dutiful to my mother, and He has not made me haughty, nor overbearing, nor arrogant, nor unblessed. And peace was upon me the day that I was born, and peace shall be upon me the day that I shall die, and on that day that I shall be raised up to life again." 19:27, 29-33

The Quran established the truth about Jesus and Mary and cleared them of all the allegations that the people had charged against them. And God honored Jesus and Mary and made them as a sign for all of humanity.

And such was Jesus, the son of Mary. This is the truth about which they still vainly doubt and dispute. 19:34

And We made the son of Mary and his mother as a sign to mankind, and symbol of Our Grace, and provided for them shelter on lofty grounds, granting them a place of rest and security, furnished with meadows and flowing streams. 23:50

Lo! Verily, this is the true account of the whole matter. And there is no God, but God, and Behold! God is indeed the Exalted in Power, in Might and is The Wise. 3:62

Mary in Islam

The Quran has 114 surahs (or chapters) and only a few of them are named after human beings. Only one is named after a woman, and that honored woman is Mary. The chapter called Surah Mariam is the nineteenth chapter in the Quran and contains 98 verses. Some of the stories shared in this surah are of Zachariah, John the Baptist, Mary, Jesus, Abraham, and others. In Islam, Mary is considered one of the most righteous women in all of humanity, and many Muslim girls are named Mariam in her honor. She is a beautiful role model for women of all faiths and her noble status is confirmed in the Quran.

Behold! The angels said, "O Mary! God hath chosen thee and purified thee and chosen thee above the women of all nations." 3:42

The Tomb of Mary is located at the foot of the Mount of Olives in Jerusalem. At one time, both Christians and Muslims shared in the care of the tomb. Still today, Muslims visit her tomb and offer prayers in her church.

The Tomb of Virgin Mary.

© 2011 Mahmoud Illean

THE CHILDREN OF ABRAHAM

Abraham, Moses, Jesus, and Mary are all loved and honored in Islam. Their stories are well known in the Muslim world and they are revered in the Islamic faith. The followers of Moses and Jesus hold a distinguished status and were given the title "The People of the Book" by virtue of the Torah and Gospel. This special relationship between Jews, Muslims, and Christians is exemplified in several places throughout the Quran.

And indeed, among the People of the Book are those who believe in God and in what was revealed to you and what was revealed to them, [being] humbly submissive to God. They do not exchange the verses of God for a small price. They will have their reward with their Lord. Indeed, God is swift in account. 3:199

Verily, those who believe, and those who are Jews, Christians or Sabians, whomsoever believeth in God and the Last Day, and who do righteous good deeds, shall have their reward with their Lord. On them, there shall be no fear, and neither shall they sorrow. 2:62

May God's peace and blessings be upon Abraham, Moses, Jesus, and Mary. And may there be peace and blessings upon all the Children of Abraham.

PROPHETS IN THE QURAN

The Quran was not only sent down as guidance but also as a validation of the earlier holy scriptures (the sacred Scrolls of Abraham, the Torah, the Psalms, and the Gospel), as well as a confirmation of many of the previous prophets and messengers that God had sent down to mankind. Muslims consider the prophets to be brothers to one another; all are given great honor, as they are among the most noble of human beings. It is believed that God has sent over 124,000 prophets and messengers throughout the history of mankind, and in the Quran, there are stories and references to 25 of them.

Given below in chronological order are their names (in both English and Arabic):

1. Adam
2. Enoch (Idris)
3. Noah (Nuh)
4. Hud*
5. Saleh*
6. Abraham (Ibrahim)
7. Lot (Lut)
8. Ishmael (Ismail)
9. Isaac (Ishaq)
10. Jacob (Yaqub)
11. Joseph (Yusuf)
12. Shu'aib*
13. Job (Ayub)

The stories of these prophets are found only in the Quran.

14. Ezekiel (Dhul-Kifl)
15. Moses (Musa)
16. Aaron (Harun)
17. David (Dawud)
18. Solomon (Sulaiman)
19. Elias/Elijah (Ilyas)
20. Elisha (Al-Yasa)
21. Jonah (Yunus)
22. Zechariah (Zakariya)
23. John the Baptist (Yahya)
24. Jesus (Isa)
25. **Muhammad

May peace and blessings be upon all of the prophets and messengers of God.

In matters of faith, He has ordained for you that religion which He commended unto Noah, and that which We inspire in you (O Muhammad) through revelation, and that which We commended unto Abraham and Moses and Jesus, saying, "Establish the religion, and be not divided therein." 42:13

** *The final prophet sent down by God, also known as the "Seal of the Prophets" is the Prophet Muhammad (peace be upon him).*

QURANIC TRANSLATIONS REFERENCED

This book is primarily focused on relating the stories of Abraham, Moses, Jesus, and Mary as told through the Quranic interpretations or translations. The following list contains ten Quranic translations that were referenced in this compilation. This collection was intentionally selected to provide a more comprehensive and nuanced expression of the verses, as some were written in the older, stylized English format (similar to the language of the Old Testament) and some in more modernized English renderings.

1. *Al-Qur'an, A Contemporary Translation*** by Ahmed Ali
2. *The Message of the Qur'an*** by Muhammad Asad
3. *English Translation and the Meaning of Al-Qur'an*** by Muhammad Farooq-i-Azam Malik
4. *The Holy Qur-an English Translation of the Meanings and Commentary* by King Fahd Holy Quran Printing
5. *Interpretation of the Meanings of the Noble Qur'an in the English Language* by Dr. Muhammad Mushin Khan
6. *The Qur'an Translation* by Abdullah Yusuf Ali
7. *The Glorious Quran* by M. Marmaduke Pickthall

** *These Quran translations are highly recommended due to their fluid writing and ease of readership.*

8. *The Holy Quran and the English Translations of the Meanings* by Arthur J. Arberry
9. *The Holy Quran with English Translation and Commentary* by Maulana Muhammad Ali
10. *The Qur'an* by M.A.S. Abdel Haleem

Most of the translations listed here also contain an author's commentary that may aid in clarification and comprehension of the text. The reader is welcome and encouraged to refer to any one of these works in order to read all of the verses that were revealed about Abraham, Moses, Jesus, and the Virgin Mary.

CLARIFYING TRANSLATIONS

The Quranic revelations were revealed in Arabic, the native language of the people of Mecca. The pre-Islamic Arab people deeply revered their language, and skilled poets, storytellers, and others who had a command of the Arabic language were often part of the most elite circles of the society.

The Quran was revealed in increments over a period of twenty-three years, given from God to Muhammad through the Angel Gabriel. During those early years of the religion, Muslims faced tremendous persecution, oppression, war and exile; later, however, they enjoyed times of peace and prosperity. Reading the verses in the context of the events that were occurring at the time of their revelation is crucial to understanding their nuanced meanings.

When the verses are read without their accompanying background information, certain verses can convey meanings that, on the surface, may seem contradictory to the overall message of the Quran. For example, a commandment that was conveyed during a time of war may take on a vastly different meaning when given during a time of peace, and vice versa.

Arabic is a rich Semitic language not unlike Aramaic and Hebrew; linguistically speaking, it is highly nuanced, with the words often having multiple meanings. A sentence may translate a certain way in one light and in another manner when looked at from another perspective. When this occurs, it is sometimes helpful to know the audience the verses were directed toward and the setting in which they were revealed. It is also helpful to remember that the Quran was sent down more than a thousand years ago, and languages and word usage can change over the centuries. What a word or phrase meant at that time may have a very different meaning in today's time. And likewise, what certain words or phrases mean now may have meant something very different when the Quran was originally sent down.

A more in-depth process in the study of the Quran is called the tafseer. In this discipline, the setting and time period, the audience the verses were directed toward, as well as the general context in which a particular surah or verse was revealed, are all examined. There are distinct levels to studying the tafseer and the deeper one goes, the more one is able to gain an understanding of the knowledge and wisdom contained within the text. All-inclusive analyses of the tafseer include close examination of historical events, the prevailing societal norms at the time, and the life stories of the people referenced in the Quran. The morals, teachings, and commandments from this work are then applied to modern times, allowing religious leaders to bridge lessons given 1,400 years ago to the issues people face in our present times.

When reading the translations of the Quran, Arabic speakers often state that the rich prose, and the splendor and beauty of the verses cannot be fully conveyed through any translated work. The people who heard the Quran at the time of its revelation were said to have been so overwhelmed and mesmerized by its language, that they were moved to tears. It is important to note that the Arab people were greatly skilled in the art of language; so much so, in fact, that in the Quran, God challenged the Arab pagans to write even one verse that can compare to the majesty of the Quran.

In this way, God challenged the disbelievers of Arabia, much as He did when He sent miracles through Moses to confront the sorcerers of his day, and through Jesus when he performed miracles in the field of healing that rivaled those of the healers of his time.

In short, trying to compare a comprehensive reading of the Quran in its original language with reading a translation of the Quran is like comparing the ocean with drops of water. There is simply no way of communicating the power and majesty of God's words other than in its original form. However, this is not to say that translations have little value. Translations are immensely and vitally important, and they do express the gist of the verses. As such, you will find many Quranic translations with various styles, in which scholars try to convey God's word to the people in their own native languages.

BOOK NOTES/ QUESTIONS FOR DISCUSSIONS

There are a few sections in the book that may be new to non-Muslim readers. Given below are a few notes that may help explain the Islamic viewpoints, which may be slightly different from the Judaic and Christian perspectives.

~ In Abraham's Chapter:

In the Quran, it is told that it was Ishmael who was being asked to be sacrificed, as he was at that time, the only son of Abraham. According to the Islamic teachings, Sarah had not yet given birth to Isaac, and Abraham's test was that much harder as he was being asked to sacrifice his only child.

~ In Mary's Chapter:

Imran was the father of the Virgin Mary, and in Islam, he is considered a prophet.

~ In the Clarifying Translations Chapter:

At the time when the Prophet Muhammad (peace be upon him) was given the Quranic revelations, the Arab people were highly skilled in the art of language and poetry. Those who had mastered this art, were considered among the most elite in the Arabian society. When God sent the Quran, the literature and language of the divine text was so beautiful on so many levels, that the people could clearly see the superiority of God's words over their own. However, their own pride and arrogance stopped them from accepting God's laws.

In a similar fashion, the sorcerers during the time of Moses (peace be upon him), were highly skilled magicians, and the most skilled were those closest to the Pharaoh and were among the most powerful members of their society. When God sent miracles and revelations to Moses (the staff, turning the river into blood, the plagues, etc.) the tests and trials were a showdown between God's true miracles and the magic tricks of the sorcerers.

Similarly, during the time of Jesus, (peace be upon him), the elite members of society were considered those who had mastered the healing arts. When Jesus healed the people (the leper, the blind, brought a bird back to life, etc.) these blessed miracles were given to show the people the true power and majesty of God's path, versus the path the people were on.

God revealed His dominion and His words through His messengers (Muhammad, Moses, Jesus) according to the cultural and societal conditions of the people so that they could easily comprehend the divine messages. God further revealed them in such manner, so as to prove beyond a shadow of a doubt the majesty and true divinity of His laws.

And in doing so, God blessed humanity with three of the greatest religions known to mankind: Judaism, Christianity, and Islam.

Questions for Discussions

Abraham, Moses, Jesus, and Mary: Divine Revelations from the Quran is one that your book club or study group may enjoy. Here are a few questions that may encourage interesting perspectives and dialogue between your members. Please feel free to use any or all of the questions in your book club or study group discussions.

~ Book Club Q&A:

1. Did any of these stories surprise you?

2. Are any of stories in this book similar to ones in the Bible or Old Testament?

3. Were there any stories that are different?

4. Which part of Abraham's stories felt most significant for you? Why?

5. Which part of Moses's stories felt most significant for you? Why?

6. Which part of Jesus's stories felt most significant for you? Why?

7. Which part of Mary's stories felt most significant for you? Why?

8. Did the "Clarifying Translations" section bring up new perspectives on Quran translations? If so, what were they?

9. Was there anything that made you feel uncomfortable or was different from your personal or faith viewpoint?

10. Do you think these three faiths share more similarities than differences or do you feel the opposite is true?

11. Do you think that these three religions come from the same source? Why or why not?

12. Do you think it is possible for Muslims, Christians, and Jews to learn from each other and perhaps work together for the betterment of humanity?

◆◆◆❖◆◆◆❖◆◆◆❖◆◆◆

ACKNOWLEDGMENTS

Many people contributed directly and indirectly to this work with their suggestions, observations, advice, and moral support. Without all of them, this book would not be in the form it is today. I'd like to first thank my husband for his generous encouragement, insights, feedback, and help in bringing this work to fruition. And to my children, thank you for your creative ideas, suggestions, awesome editing and for being my sounding board. You are the inspiration for everything I do, and being your mother is the greatest joy in my life.

Thank you also to my mother who taught me the importance of Islam, and to my father who taught me the value of character. And to my brother, sister, sister-in-law, and my two fun-loving nephews– thank you for making life more beautiful. I love you all. May your lives be filled with much happiness and peace.

FINAL THOUGHTS

The deep and powerful love God showers upon Abraham, Moses, Jesus, and Mary is self-evident when one reads the beautiful verses about them in the Quran. My intention in writing this book was to share a tiny bit of that love and beauty with those who may not be as familiar with the Quran. I hope in some small way, I was able to do that.

Whatever benefit one may find in this book comes solely from God. And whatever mistakes there are in this book are due to my own oversights, and I ask for forgiveness from God and from my readers for those.

May God bless us all with His grace and mercy. May He grant us guidance and happiness. And may our hearts be filled with contentment and our lives with joy and peace.

May peace be upon you– *Assalamu Alaikum.*

Thasneem Ahmed

Dear Reader,

Thank you for sharing your time and reading "Abraham, Moses, Jesus, and Mary: Divine Revelations from the Quran." I sincerely hope you enjoyed the book and found it interesting. I'd love to hear your thoughts and would be honored if you could leave a review on Amazon. Thank you again. Together, we can bring more peace and understanding to the world...

Kind regards,
Thasneem

To see more of Thasneem's work, please visit:
www.faithandrevelations.com

www.ingramcontent.com/pod-product-compliance
Lightning Source LLC
Chambersburg PA
CBHW071639050426
42443CB00026B/771